Sinkholes

Nadia Higgins

rourkeeducationalmedia.com

Scan for Related Titles
and Teacher Resources

Before Reading:

Building Academic Vocabulary and Background Knowledge

Before reading a book, it is important to tap into what your child or students already know about the topic. This will help them develop their vocabulary, increase their reading comprehension, and make connections across the curriculum.

1. *Look at the cover of the book. What will this book be about?*
2. *What do you already know about the topic?*
3. *Let's study the Table of Contents. What will you learn about in the book's chapters?*
4. *What would you like to learn about this topic? Do you think you might learn about it from this book? Why or why not?*
5. *Use a reading journal to write about your knowledge of this topic. Record what you already know about the topic and what you hope to learn about the topic.*
6. *Read the book.*
7. *In your reading journal, record what you learned about the topic and your response to the book.*
8. *After reading the book complete the activities below.*

Content Area Vocabulary
Read the list. What do these words mean?

bedrock
collapse sinkholes
drought
groundwater
imploding
insurance
karst area
oases
particles
porous
radar
subsidence sinkholes

After Reading:

Comprehension and Extension Activity

After reading the book, work on the following questions with your child or students in order to check their level of reading comprehension and content mastery.

1. *Can sinkholes be a positive thing? Explain.* (Summarize)
2. *Why is limestone a cause of many sinkholes?* (Infer)
3. *What is the importance of groundwater for people and the Earth?* (Asking questions)
4. *How can humans fix or prevent sinkholes?* (Summarize)
5. *Why are geologists an important piece when talking about sinkholes?* (Infer)

Extension Activity

For hundreds of years people have created stories, like myths and legends, to explain natural disasters. Research the differences between myths and legends. Then think of a story that would explain why sinkholes happen. Write that story in the format of a myth or legend and share with your classmates or teacher.

Table of Contents

Get Out of the Building!

"I'm definitely haunted by that night," Maggie Ghamry said. The date was August 11, 2013. Maggie was vacationing at the Summer Bay Resort in Clermont, Florida, just down the road from Walt Disney World. It was a typical August evening at the resort. Tourists in tank tops and flip flops settled into their rooms. Energetic children slammed doors and ran up and down the halls.

Florida is known as the Sunshine State. These days, it's also gaining fame as the nation's sinkhole capital.

At first, Maggie figured that the commotion she was hearing was just some kids outside her door. The floor shook, and there were strange popping noises. Then she heard windows breaking. "Next thing I knew, people are yelling, 'Get out of the building! Get out the building!'" Maggie said.

The evacuation of the Summer Bay Resort started at about 10:30 p.m. The disaster seemed to come out of nowhere. In reality, the sinkhole had been forming for years underground.

Some people threw their belongings off balconies before they rushed out. One woman ran straight from the tub when it bounced into the air. Another couple's door wouldn't open because the frame collapsed. They climbed out of their window with their baby.

"It almost seemed like the building was **imploding,** turning in a vortex, as if being consumed in quicksand. It was so surreal," Maggie said.

As everyone fled, one person rushed from room to room. Security guard Richard Shanley remembers the ceiling falling down around him as he ran through the halls, searching for stragglers. Thanks to Richard, all 36 guests escaped the building shaken but unharmed. Some 40 minutes later, the three-story building crumbled into a sinkhole the size of a football field.

Fast Fact

Sinkholes are also known as sinks, swallow holes, and dolines.

What Is a Sinkhole?

If you live in Florida, you may have heard sinkhole stories. The state gets more sinkholes than just about any other place on Earth, about 17 per day. But even for native Floridians, the sinkhole at Summer Bay Resort was a shock.

A sinkhole is a lot like what it sounds like. The surface layer of the Earth sinks into an underground hole. Thankfully, though, these events are usually slow-moving. You might notice a sinkhole growing for months or years. The sinkhole at Summer Bay Resort was a terrifying exception.

This collapse sinkhole in a salt dome opened in Daisetta, Texas, in 2008. Salt can dissolve rapidly, which leads to large, bowl-shaped craters. In this case, the injection of fluids into the salt dome caused a 60 foot (18.3 meter) sinkhole to open. It covered multiple acres and destroyed several structures.

9

Luckily, no one died that August day. Once in a great while, a sinkhole can be deadly. In February 2013, a sinkhole opened up under Jeff Bush's bedroom floor in Seffner, Florida.

An overhead view of Jeff Bush's ruined home shows the sinkhole that opened up under his bed. Here, officials have filled the deadly sinkhole with crushed rock.

At the sound of screams, Jeremy Bush ran to his brother's room, flung open the door, and turned on the light. "All I saw was this big, massive hole," he said. Jeff Bush had been swallowed up as he slept in his bed. The hole was so deep, he was gone forever.

Jeff Bush was only the fourth person ever to be killed by a Florida sinkhole. Unlike other natural disasters, sinkholes are localized. To get hurt, you pretty much have to be on top of a sinkhole when it collapses. In fact, the odds of getting killed by a sinkhole are far lower than getting struck by lightning.

Jeff Bush's bizarre and sudden death was especially shocking to his brother, Jeremy Bush, who was also home when the sinkhole collapsed. Here, Jeremy and Rachel Wicker grieve for Jeff at at a memorial service.

As Florida farmers pumped large amounts of water to protect their plants from a hard freeze in 2010, the groundwater levels dipped so low that more than 110 sinkholes formed in the Dover area.

Huge Headaches

More often, sinkholes are just huge headaches. The holes are hard to predict, and they are difficult and expensive to repair. If a sinkhole develops under your house, it can crack the walls, ruin the plumbing, or worse. In sinkhole areas, homeowners pay for costly **insurance** to protect them if a sinkhole opens up on their property.

About 20 homeowners lost their homes when the sinkholes opened up in Dover. The sinkholes also destroyed roads and some agricultural areas.

Fast Fact

Sinkholes are most common in Alabama, Florida, Kentucky, Missouri, Pennsylvania, Tennessee, and Texas.

Sinkholes also damage roads and create havoc with underground sewers and cables. Many sinkholes are like giant drains. They connect to freshwater reserves under the ground. Pollution that drips down a sinkhole can leak into the **groundwater**. That unsafe water could end up in someone's drinking glass.

Workers repair an underground pipe that brings drinking water to people's homes.

Fast Fact

Groundwater is a big deal. There's 100 times more water stored underground than there is in all of Earth's lakes and rivers.

Natural Treasures

Sinkholes happen in almost every state and every country. You may have seen a sinkhole and not even realized it. A sinkhole can seem like a valley that stretches for miles, or it may just be a grassy dip in a field.

A sparkling lake or quiet pond could be a sinkhole that filled with water. Many lush, green **oases** started when sinkholes tapped into groundwater below the desert sands.

A sinkhole feeds water to an oasis in the desert of Oman, a country in the Middle East.

A sinkhole may be so small, you could have dug it yourself. Or it can be so deep, you can't even see to the bottom. Some sinkholes look like Moon craters. Others are vast, rocky caverns. They carry the echoes of rare creatures who thrive in damp, dark places.

Sinkholes have been carving out Earth's landscape for millions of years. Before they were natural disasters, they played an important role in human history. Prehistoric people used sinkholes as animal traps. The early hunters drove their prey into the holes, where they could be easily snatched.

The ancient Mayan people built their cities around Mexico's water-filled sinkholes, called cenotes. The cenotes were more than just important water sources. Mayans considered the beautiful spots sacred.

These days, tourists still flock to Mexico's cenotes to dive and swim in the freshwater pools. When it comes to sinkholes, location is everything. Sinkholes can be fun, strange, terrifying, or just the worst hassle ever. It all depends on what's around them when they start to sink.

Two Kinds of Sinkholes

About 10 percent of the Earth's surface is made up of terrain that is sensitive to sinkhole formation. What make these places special? The answer lies underground, in the layer of rock that stretches under the soil. Sinkholes form where the **bedrock** is soft.

Often, that bedrock is limestone, as it is in Florida. Rain trickles down through the soil and seeps into the soft rock. Little by little, the rain dissolves the rock. It chisels out underground cracks, channels, and holes. Water pools in the holes, and they grow into caverns. As the bedrock starts to look like Swiss cheese, it creates a **karst area**.

Usually limestone bedrock cannot be seen because it is under soil. Here, exposed limestone shows how rainwater shapes the soft rock in a karst area.

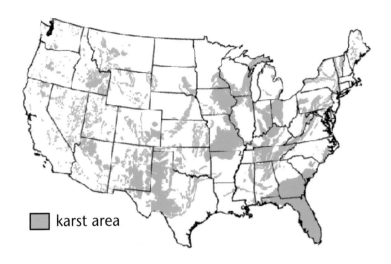

karst area

This map shows where soft bedrock lies under soil in the United States. These areas are most prone to sinkholes. Notice how green Florida is!

People's steps can trigger a sinkhole even under a concrete sidewalk.

Fast Fact

About one-fifth of the United States sits on bedrock that can cause sinkholes.

Slowly Sinking

Authorities aren't taking any chances with this sinkhole. They've closed the road and blocked it off on all sides so nobody drives over it.

Two main kinds of sinkholes develop in a karst area. **Subsidence sinkholes** are far more common. They develop slowly. As an underground cavern grows, soil spills down from above to fill it. The looser the soil, the better it flows. As the cavern keeps growing, more soil spills down. The ground's surface starts to slump.

How Subsidence Sinkholes Form

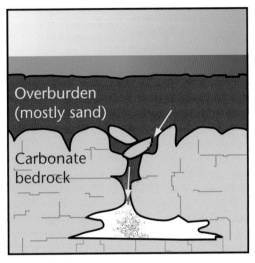

1. Sandy soil begins spilling into cracks in the soft bedrock.

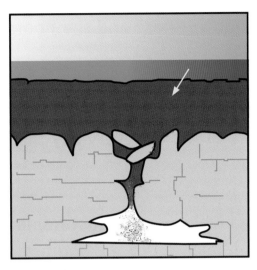

2. More soil spills down and the cracks continue to open up.

3. The ground above begins to slump as soil spills into the bedrock.

4. A subsidence sinkhole slowly develops.

Dean and Heather Williams have a subsidence sinkhole growing under their house in Bartow, Florida. As the house slowly sinks down, cracks are growing in the walls. The windows shake and the floors make popping noises.

The Williams family would like to buy a new house, but they don't have the money. And, without insurance, repairs would cost $100,000! Every day they wonder, *Is this the day the house falls in?*

"I feel like we're just riding on the Titanic," Dean Williams said, referring to the doomed ship of 1911. "We're just waiting for the iceberg."

The roots of this tree collapsed because of subsidence activity. Subsidence is the motion of the Earth's surface as it shifts downward. Land subsidence happens when large amounts of groundwater are withdrawn from certain areas.

In 2014, a collapse sinkhole opened up under the National Corvette Museum in Bowling Green, Kentucky. Eight rare Corvettes fell into a 30 foot (9 meter) hole.

Swallowed Up!

This collapse sinkhole opened up near Frederick, Maryland, in 2003. Sinkholes often develop near and under roadways because of the concentration of rainwater runoff in storm drains and ditches nearby.

Collapse sinkholes are the dramatic ones that make the news. In this case, the soil starts to spill down into a bedrock cavern. But the soil on top is sticky. It doesn't flow very well. This soil forms a roof over the growing hole beneath it. The roof gets thinner and thinner until — crash! It caves in all at once.

How Collapse Sinkholes Form

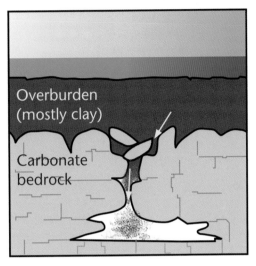

Overburden (mostly clay)

Carbonate bedrock

1. Soil begins to spill into a hole in the bedrock.

2. The soil near the top doesn't flow down. Instead it forms a roof over the hole.

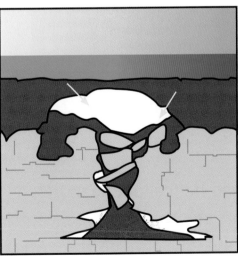

3. The soil roof gets thinner as the hole grows under it.

4. The soil roof gets so thin it collapses when something shakes it.

Carla Chapman, from southern Florida, fell into a collapse sinkhole in her own backyard. Carla was outside gardening when a scampering lizard startled her and she jumped back. The force of her landing set off a collapse sinkhole. The next thing she knew, she was standing in a dirt hole that went higher than her head.

Carla Chapman's husband, Keith, shows the sinkhole that almost swallowed his wife. The hole is barely wider than a person's shoulders!

"There wasn't any grass. There wasn't anything to hold on to. It was wet clay, this heavy clay," Carla remembered. "I know what it feels like to begin to suffocate, and the harder you struggle, the further down you go."

Fast Fact

Only one to two percent of sinkholes are collapse sinkholes.

Carla had her cellphone in her pocket, but she couldn't get reception underground. She thought fast. She dialed 911, threw her phone out of the hole, and screamed for help. Her plan worked, and emergency workers rescued her unharmed.

Sinkhole in a Jar

Try this experiment to see how a sinkhole forms.

What you need:

- a large jar
- enough dirt to fill the jar
- a toilet paper tube
- flour
- water

Steps:

1. Place the toilet paper roll inside the jar.
2. Fill up the space around the toilet paper roll with dirt. Try not to get dirt inside the roll, and fill the jar only to the top of the roll.
3. Fill the roll with flour.
4. Carefully remove the toilet paper roll from the jar.
5. Continue filling the jar with dirt. Leave about an inch of empty space at the top.
6. Top off the jar with water. Let the water settle in and watch the dirt's surface cave in!

What happened?

The water was like rain, and the flour was like limestone. The water dissolved the flour. It made a hole, and the dirt fell into it.

Sinkhole Triggers

Often, a sinkhole needs a trigger to set it off. Construction crews begin building on it, or a car drives over it. In Carla's case, her own footsteps were the trigger.

The Role of Water

Water greatly affects how fast sinkholes form and collapse. Heavy rains can speed up a sinkhole by washing away soil **particles**. The soil above a hole gets even thinner.

Too little water can pose danger, too. During a **drought**, the particles in soil shrink and separate. So when rain does eventually come, it easily causes the dry, brittle earth to crash down.

Sinkholes can be repaired in various ways. Some require injecting the hole with grout, which is a mixture of cement, sand, water, and sometimes gravel.

A Mining Disaster

Human activity is another significant contributor to sinkholes. Just ask the 350 residents of Bayou Corne, Louisiana. Their small town has been taken over by a swampy sinkhole that opened up in August 2012.

A salt mining company had drilled too close to the edge of an underground salt dome. The fragile mine collapsed, causing a sinkhole. In turn, that unlocked underground stores of explosive gas and oil, which started spewing from the hole.

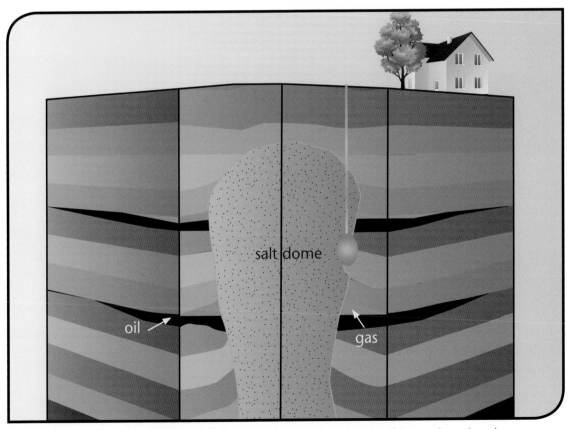

A salt dome is a rock-like structure formed under the Earth's surface by the upward movement of a mass of salt. When the Bayou Corne mine walls buckled, gas and oil in the ground escaped into the town's air.

Two years later, the sinkhole was as wide as about 20 football fields. It plunged down 750 feet (229 meters), about the height of a 75-story skyscraper. The sinkhole will continue to grow for years, experts say. Most people have evacuated the town. It stinks like gasoline, and residents worry about the oil and gas starting fires or polluting the groundwater.

"How often do you see a tree go straight down?"
- Bayou Corne resident John Boudreaux

From above, the Bayou Corne sinkhole looks like a peaceful lake, not the sucking swamp it really is.

More Human Triggers

City plumbing is another human activity that can trigger a sinkhole. In 2010, a sinkhole opened in the heart of Guatemala City, in the Republic of Guatemala. It sucked a three-story building 300 feet (91 meters) down. Heavy rain was a trigger, but a leaky sewer had also weakened the soil and rock under the building.

Guatemala City's 2010 sinkhole swallowed a three-story factory right in the middle of a crowded neighborhood.

Farmers in sinkhole areas also have to be careful watering their crops. They don't want to draw too quickly from groundwater supplies. That groundwater could be filling underground holes, and holding up the soil. When that water gets sucked away, the soil crashes down.

This sinkhole in a Florida strawberry field was filled in with dirt after it opened up in 2010.

Developers in Florida are always thinking about how their plans will affect sinkholes. Even something as simple as cutting down a tree could cause trouble. The tree's roots could be holding the soil together.

Parking lots, roads, and driveways need to be thought through, too. They change the natural flow of water along the ground. Rainwater doesn't sink through a paved surface. Instead, it runs off along the edges. Extra waterfall all in one place could speed up a sinkhole.

A sinkhole hidden under a flooded roadway can be disastrous for drivers.

What Can Be Done

What's the best way to avoid a sinkhole? Don't build a house or road on top of an underground cavern in the first place. That sounds obvious, but it's easier said than done.

Underground Clues

Geologists have several ways of looking for sinkhole signs underground. They use **radar** to send waves deep into the Earth. By tracking how the waves change direction, scientists get a sense of underground cracks and holes.

Gravity provides another search method. The force of Earth's gravity shifts slightly in a limestone cavern. A gravimeter can detect these tiny shifts.

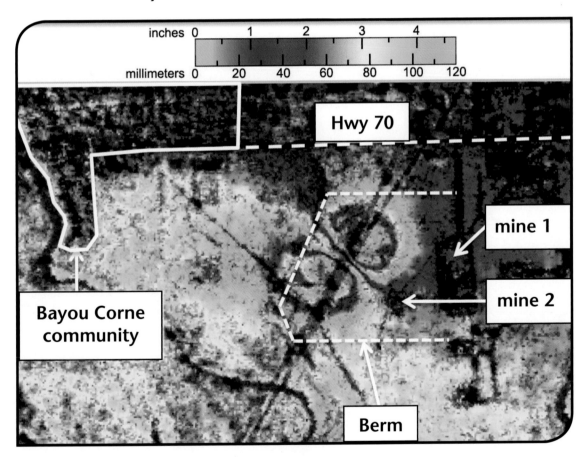

An analysis by NASA's Uninhabited Aerial Vehicle Synthetic Aperture Radar (UAVSAR) after the sinkhole formed in Bayou Corne, Louisiana, indicated that ground movement was detected more than a month before the collapse. The colors in the analysis show surface movement.

During a sinkhole test, experts may drill deep underground to collect rock and soil samples. They analyze these materials, looking for telltale patterns. They figure out how water is flowing underground. Back at their computers, geologists put all their clues together to create maps of the ground under our feet.

Fast Fact

A sinkhole test on a single backyard can cost from $5,000 to $10,000.

A geologist collects soil from a hole. He'll take the soil back to a lab for further study.

Be a Sinkhole Sleuth

You can be on the lookout for sinkholes, too. Look for these common signs:

- ☑ Areas in your lawn or garden that seem to be dying for no reason. Water could be draining down a sinkhole.

- ☑ Slumping sign posts and trees

- ☑ Doors that won't shut because the frame is skewed

- ☑ Cracks in walls or along the foundation of a building

- ☑ Muddy well water

- ☑ New ponds forming after rainfall

Sinkhole Fixes

Many people move out if a sinkhole is growing on their property. Filling a sinkhole can cost nearly as much as buying a new house. Also, sinkhole repair disrupts the ground. The process of fixing a small hole can trigger an even bigger one. That's what happened to Joan and Jim Bates of Spring Hill, Florida. Their entire house collapsed as crews tried to save it.

Cracks along the exterior of a home can indicate sinkhole activity on the property. Deep cracks in sidewalks and driveways also can signal subsidence damage.

Even so, sinkhole repair is becoming a booming business, and methods are improving. One successful strategy is to drill out a cavity all the way to the bedrock. Crews then fill the hole with layers of boulders, rocks, and sand. That creates a stable but **porous** surface. Rainwater can run through without soaking any one spot.

Crews may also bolt a building down. They run steel pipes straight from the house, through the soil, and into the bedrock below. This idea is similar to a beach house that sits on stilts. It doesn't matter if the soil shifts. The house stays grounded.

City workers repair a water pipe inside a sinkhole. They need to take extreme care so their actions don't trigger another sinkhole or make this one larger.

Record Breakers

Here are some of the most amazing sinkholes of all time. These record breakers from all over the world show just how spooky and spectacular sinkholes can be.

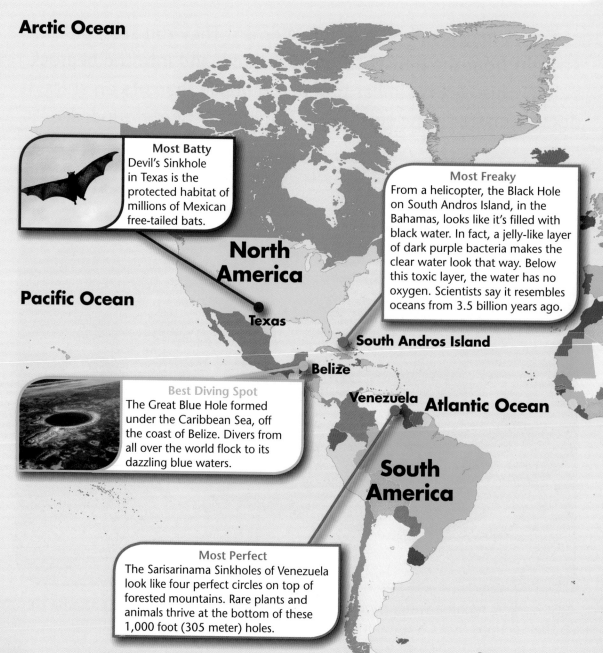

Arctic Ocean

Most Batty
Devil's Sinkhole in Texas is the protected habitat of millions of Mexican free-tailed bats.

North America

Pacific Ocean

Texas

Most Freaky
From a helicopter, the Black Hole on South Andros Island, in the Bahamas, looks like it's filled with black water. In fact, a jelly-like layer of dark purple bacteria makes the clear water look that way. Below this toxic layer, the water has no oxygen. Scientists say it resembles oceans from 3.5 billion years ago.

South Andros Island

Belize

Venezuela

Atlantic Ocean

Best Diving Spot
The Great Blue Hole formed under the Caribbean Sea, off the coast of Belize. Divers from all over the world flock to its dazzling blue waters.

South America

Most Perfect
The Sarisarinama Sinkholes of Venezuela look like four perfect circles on top of forested mountains. Rare plants and animals thrive at the bottom of these 1,000 foot (305 meter) holes.

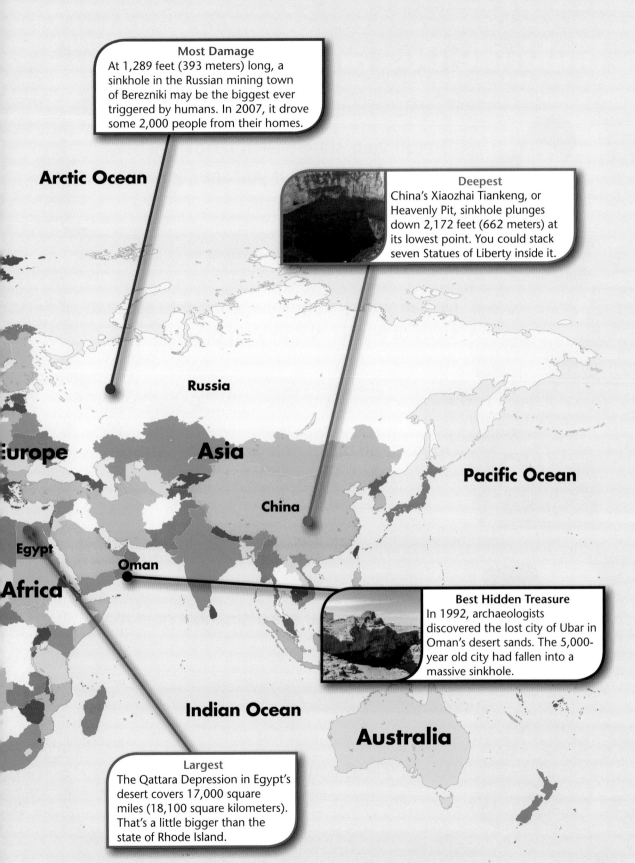

Most Damage
At 1,289 feet (393 meters) long, a sinkhole in the Russian mining town of Bereznki may be the biggest ever triggered by humans. In 2007, it drove some 2,000 people from their homes.

Arctic Ocean

Deepest
China's Xiaozhai Tiankeng, or Heavenly Pit, sinkhole plunges down 2,172 feet (662 meters) at its lowest point. You could stack seven Statues of Liberty inside it.

Russia

Europe

Asia

Pacific Ocean

China

Egypt

Oman

Africa

Best Hidden Treasure
In 1992, archaeologists discovered the lost city of Ubar in Oman's desert sands. The 5,000-year old city had fallen into a massive sinkhole.

Indian Ocean

Australia

Largest
The Qattara Depression in Egypt's desert covers 17,000 square miles (18,100 square kilometers). That's a little bigger than the state of Rhode Island.

Sinkhole Dos and Don'ts

 Do call your state's DNR (Department of Natural Resources) if you see signs of a sinkhole on public land.

 Do call your insurance agent if you suspect signs of a sinkhole on your property.

 Do mark off a sinkhole with tape or rope to warn others.

 Do call 911 if you see a sinkhole on a road.

 Do call 911 if you see a sinkhole collapsing.

 Do evacuate, if necessary.

 Don't put garbage in a sinkhole! It can lead directly to your drinking water supply.

 Do call your state's DNR if you see a sinkhole filled with trash.

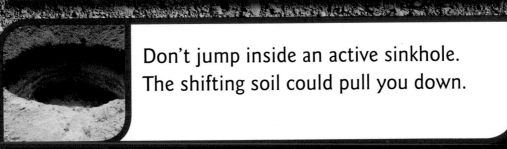 Don't jump inside an active sinkhole. The shifting soil could pull you down.

Glossary

bedrock (BED-rawk): the layer of rock that lies underground beneath the soil

collapse sinkholes (kuh-LAPS SINK-holz): sinkholes that cave in all at once

drought (DROUT): a long period without rain or snow

groundwater (GROUND-wah-tuhr): fresh water held between spaces in the soil or bedrock

imploding (ihm-PLO-ding): caving in

insurance (in-SHOOR-ens): an agreement where someone pays money in exchange for protection in case of a disaster

karst area (KAHRST AIR-ee-uh): an area of land where the bedrock has many tunnels, cracks, and caverns

oases (oh-AY-seez): places in the desert where a water source lets plants grow

particles (PART-ih-kuhlz): grains

porous (PAWR-uhs): full of many small holes

radar (RAY-dar): technology that uses reflected waves to map out unseen objects

subsidence sinkholes (SUB-sih-dens SINK-holz): sinkholes that slump down slowly

Index

Show What You Know

1. What are the two main types of sinkholes, and how are they different?
2. Give an example of a sinkhole that has been valued by humans.
3. How do geologists look for sinkhole clues underground?
4. Name one human activity that can trigger a sinkhole.
5. How might you know if a sinkhole is growing under your yard?

Websites to Visit

www.pbskids.org/dragonflytv/show/sinkholes.html
www.10mosttoday.com/10-most-amazing-sinkholes-in-the-world
www.geography.about.com/od/hazardsanddisasters/a/sinkholes.html

About the Author

Nadia Higgins is the author of more than 80 books for children and young adults. She has written about everything from ants to zombies. Her favorite part of being a writer is doing research and finding odd facts that will amaze her readers. Ms. Higgins lives in Minneapolis, Minnesota, with her husband and two daughters.

Meet The Author!
www.meetREMauthors.com

www.rourkeeducationalmedia.com

PHOTO CREDITS: Cover © Brian Peterson/ZUMA Press/Corbis; Title Page © dschreiber29; page 4 © Paul Giamou, Cheryl Graham; page 5,6,7 © John Raoux/AP/Corbis; page 8,9, 26 © U.S. Geological Survey/Randall Orndorff; page 10 © Dirk Shadd/ ASSOCIATED PRESS; page 11 © Daniel Wallace/ASSOCIATED PRESS; page 12,13, 24,34,39,40 © U.S. Geological Survey/Ann Tihansky; page 14 © Mike Clarke; page 15 © brianeasley; page 16 © slobo; page 17 © Jose Ignasio Soto; page 18 © SUMATUSCANI; page 19 © Justin McDonald; page 20 © willyseto; page 21 © U.S. Geological Survey, daizuoxin; page 22 © Shaun Lowe; page 23,27,31 © Jen Thomas; page 25 © Michael Noble Jr./AP/Corbis; page 28 © Ileana Morales/ZUMA Press/Corbis; page 29 © Jamesmcq24, ozgurdonmaz, Jurgen Francois, AlasdairJames, t_kimura; page 30 © tfoxfoto; page 32 © Julie Dermansky/Corbis; page 33 © DANIEL LECLAIR/Reuters/Corbis; page 35 © RapidEye; page 36 © Tammy Bryngelson; page 37 © NASA/JPL-Caltech; page 38 © lizia; page 41 © DnHolm; page 42, 43 © Pingebat; page 42 © CraigRJD, Mlenny; page 43 © Brookqi, Gunter Hoffman; page 44 © Jane Norton, BartCo, Daniel Timiras, F. und T. Werner, Carly1050; page 45 © FredericoC, silverjohn, seraficus, Big hole

Edited by: Keli Sipperley
Cover and interior design by: Jen Thomas

Library of Congress PCN Data

Sinkholes / Nadia Higgins
(Devastating Disasters)
  ISBN 978-1-63430-422-1 (hard cover)
  ISBN 978-1-63430-522-8 (soft cover)
  ISBN 978-1-63430-612-6 (e-Book)
Library of Congress Control Number: 2015931735

Also Available as:

Rourke's e-Books